Roger B. Penn, Jr.

Not Everything Is
Purple

Stable Hill Press ✺ Portland, OR

Not Everything Is Purple

for

Mona & Lisa Wagner

Who make the world groovy

and

Isabeau Waia'u Walker

He kukui nani

Observations

The Box Was Full Once

the box was full once
I've broken so many crayons since then
I can still color brilliantly
in black and white

like a questing bee
I sampled tulips
daffodils
lilacs
buttercups
daisies
before slowing down to smell the
roses
now I can barely recall
the forget-me-nots

meanwhile
the world keeps on spinning
while I fly off on a tangent
like space junk

Candlelight

I'm writing these lines
by candlelight
flickering thoughts
cast dancing shadows of imagination
on the ceiling

I'm writing these lines
by candlelight
the words aglow with
shifting hues of
meaning

I'm writing these lines
by candlelight
a glimmering conscience
bravely defying
the night

I'm writing these lines
by candlelight
that dimly illuminates
the corners of my mind
where fading memories hide
like worn-out words
sentenced to death

Wildflowers

yesterday we were wildflowers
watching the needles
of the playful pine trees
sprinkle themselves on
grass
moist with poetry
and a water bug danced
to the fragrant melody
of the strawberry brook

then
without warning
stars became storm

this morning
the sun was afraid
to rise
and here in the cold dark
one lone petal
lies melting
in the rain

Blue

It was a dark blue Thursday
the rain had grown
weary; the pavement still
slick
shadows emerged
...timidly
lurking in the mist

stepping over a puddle and
turning the corner
slowly it became clear
that some days
even the sun is
blue

Together

two lambent stars
found a new constellation
an exquisite harmony
da Vinci never imagined
euphonic reincarnations
spilling earthward
like sonorous rain
when they're together
orange happens

a voice far from home

connecting souls with six strings

he pōmaika'i

the Cottage

tears falling
from weeping fuchsias
under a pine umbrella
the scent of
earnest conversation
mingling with the sound
of coffee
ardently savored
with chocolate, biscotti,
and sighs
the warmth of laughter and
companionship
the dreary December chill
cannot penetrate

Christmas Lane

the snow settled hopefully
on Christmas Lane
the peaceful hush
of fragrant fir trees
and the scent of white

the anticipation of gingerbread
and cocoa intensifies the
brightening darkness
encouraging snowmen to
come out of hiding
and wave at the occasional car
treading carefully on the
newly fallen carpet

shafts of warm light
beckon from frosty windows
bedecked in twinkling colors
secretly signaling to an
impending sleigh

Six Feet from Everywhere

hiding under a cloth pretense
not knowing who I am
adrift in a churning sea of
lifeless eyes
yearning for something
unrevealed

six feet from everywhere
remnants of humanity
relegated to
stupefaction

Wings

Snug in my comfortable nest
Afraid to try my
Imagination
Yet longing to sing

Finally
Gathering my courage
I spread my mind
And fly

Purple

not everything is purple
some things sound like
rabbits giggling
in a fresh snow

smell like dandelion milk
and taste like moonbeams
tickling a dark forest

some things feel like velvet
rubbed the wrong way
or hedgehogs
playing twister

not everything is purple
some things can only
pretend

autopilot

milepost 162
mountaintops in view
hairpin turns make the going slow
so many miles to go

milepost 163
the pavement sings to me
getting hard to stay awake
wishing I could take a break

milepost 164
how many miles more?
hawks and sparrows watch me drive by
wondering why I don't fly

milepost 165
humming along in overdrive
weariness starting to take its toll
hour by hour toward my goal

milepost 167
wait...what?

Success

Treading water in a cesspool of apathy
Nurturing dreams of stagnation
The frantic pursuit of ennui fueled by
Aspirations of mediocrity
Ultimately to be mired in complacency
The fossilized remains of abandoned ambitions
Now on display in the Museum
of Natural Misery

A 2020 Christmas

Santa loaded up his sleigh
With lots of extra alcohol
It wasn't for consumption;
He didn't drink at all

But no viruses could linger
On the gifts he left behind
So he carefully wiped down every one
Just to give them peace of mind

The foggy parts were tricky
Rudolph's nose did little good
Its light was hidden behind a mask
But he tried the best he could

So many tempting cookies
Frosty milk he couldn't touch
To find their treats untasted
Wouldn't please them very much

The presents he could hardly see
He hoped he got them right
But his mask fogged up his glasses
And it didn't help his sight

Still, the one gift that he gave to all
He knew would bring good cheer
The hope that things would soon be right
And a better year next year

traffic

physics doesn't account for
traffic
where an object in motion tends to
stay at rest
going nowhere
at the speed of halt

the insistent rain
trying in vain
to wash away
the amassed vehicular detritus

the windshield wipers applauding
the performance of a
choir of brake lights
singing in morse code

Luz

From a little farm in
Paso Canoas
the gateway to the land of
coffee and
pineapple

To the sands of Puntarenas
the benevolent sun painted the trees
and flowers with
watercolors, rum, and splashes
of mango

Elsewhere
the light of Alajuelita
smelled like sunshine and guanabana
made my pulse beat a merengue
and set the darkest nights
on fire

dawn reverie

your liquid smile
lingers
in my coffee

steamy tendrils of
your warm breath
caress my face

the subtle flavor of
your kiss
in the cup makes
my lips
tremble
with desire